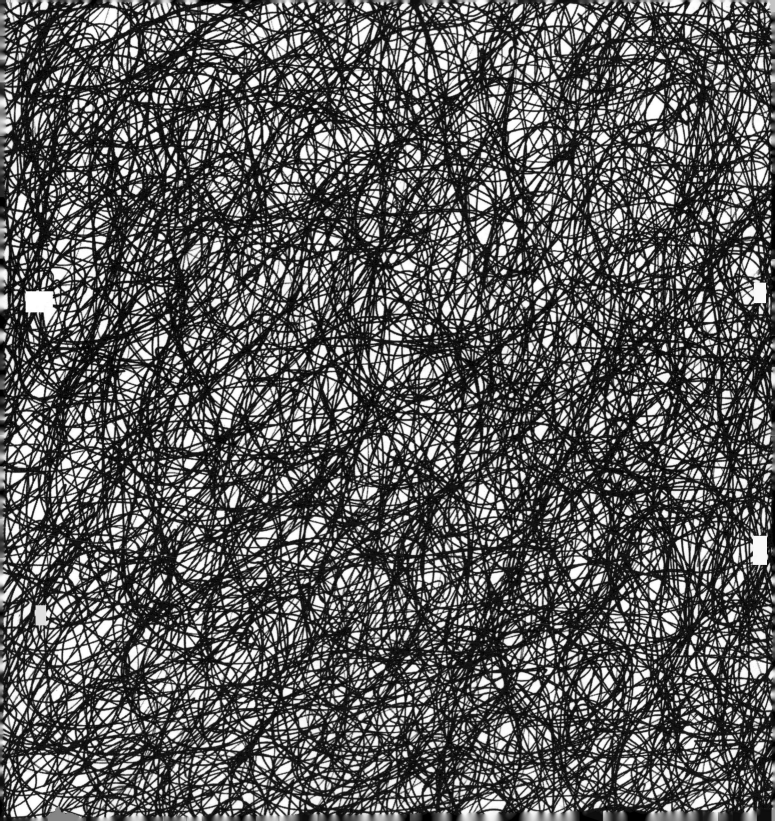

Scribble Art

A how-to guide and coloring book

Written & Scribbled by
Tish McAllise Sjoberg

Art Helps Art Heals Publishing
San Diego, CA 92104
TheScribbleBook.com

First Edition
Printed in the United States of America

Book design and illustrations by Tish McAllise Sjoberg

ISBN-13: 978-0692623497 (Art Helps Art Heals)
ISBN-10: 0692623493

Dedicated to my son, Shea,
who taught me in his early years
that scribbling is our first art form.
And, to my Expressive Arts clients
who scribble their hearts out
to find expression and peace.

The scribble.

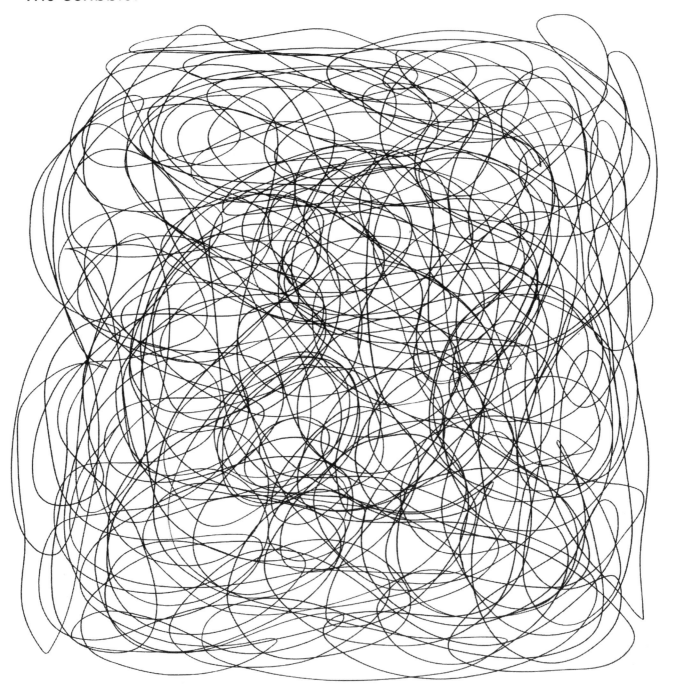

The simplest of all art forms.

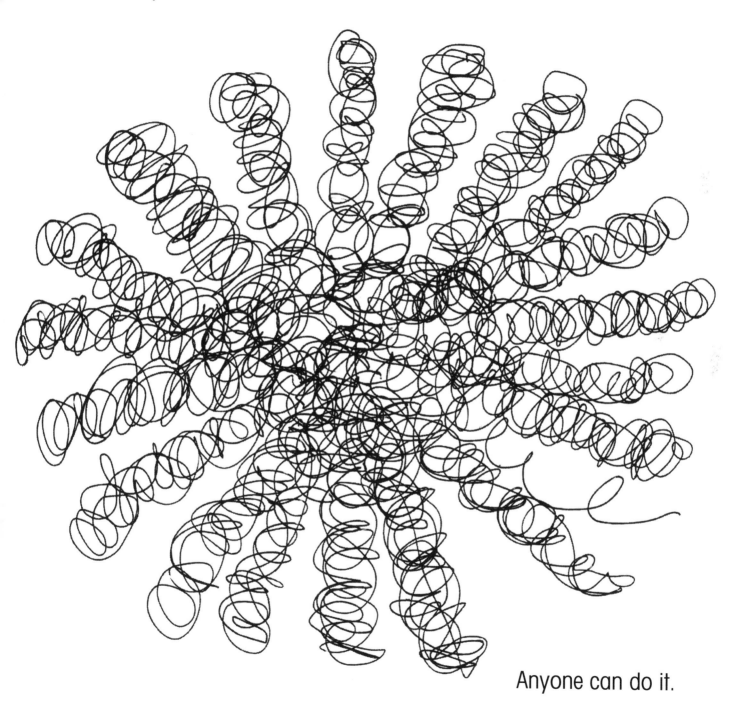

Anyone can do it.

You don't need any special talent or tools,

just a piece of paper and a pen.

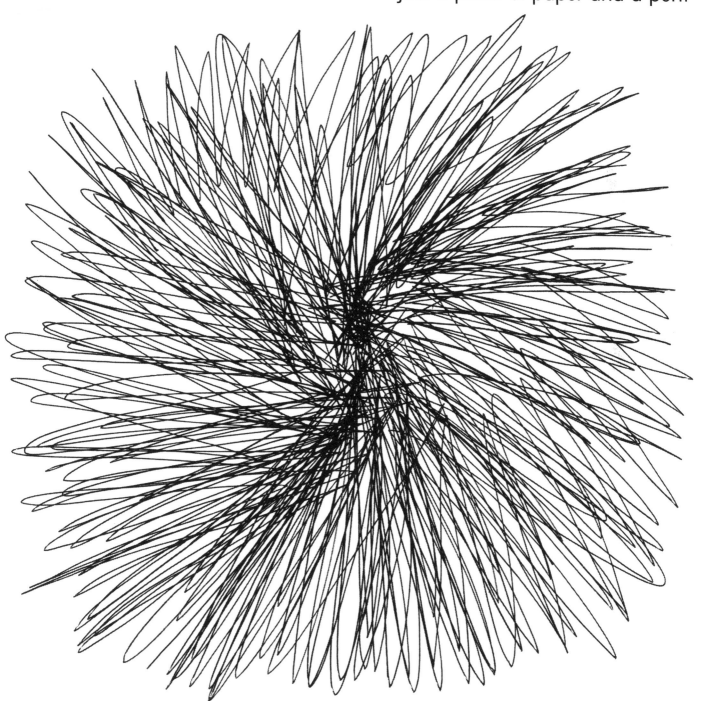

Touch the pen to the paper, and let it move around the page.

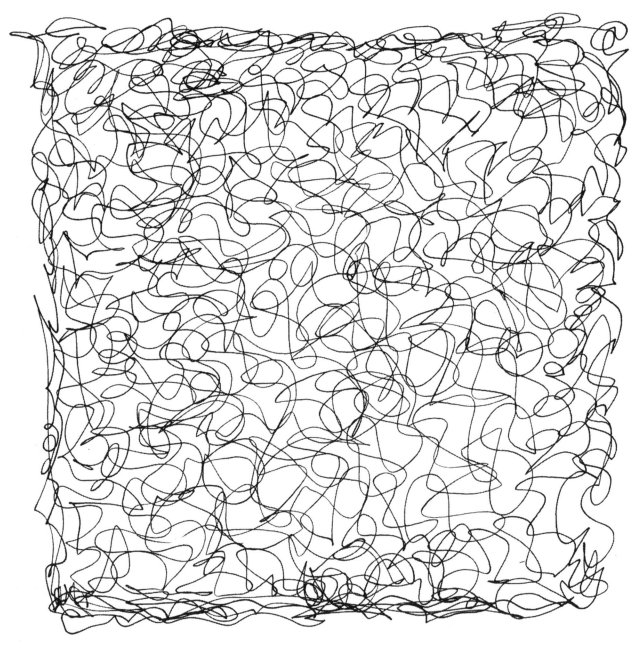

Don't stop—keep going.

When you stop, sometimes you start thinking.

A scribble is a non-thinking
activity.

You are not drawing anything.

You are just scribbling
and scribbling and scribbling.

The scribble is so simple to do, yet it can be very satisfying.

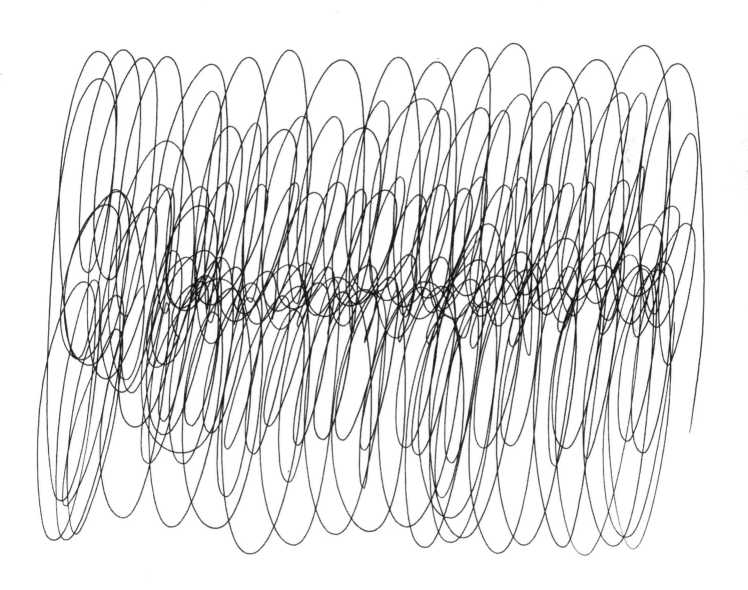

You can put your feelings and emotions behind your scribble.

Scribble an angry scribble.

A sad scribble.

A happy scribble.

Scribble an anxious scribble.

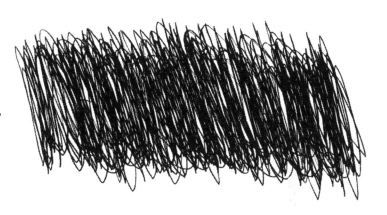

A nervous scribble.

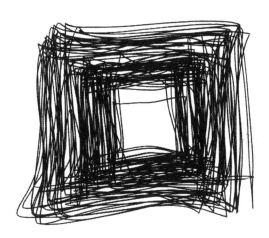

A peaceful scribble.

There is something gratifying about seeing the expression
of that emotion on the paper.

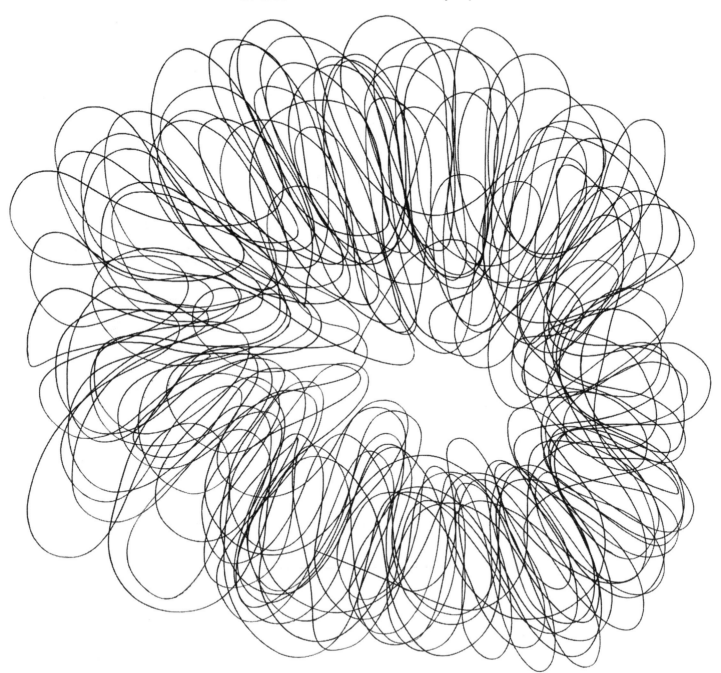

Or turning that emotion into something artful.

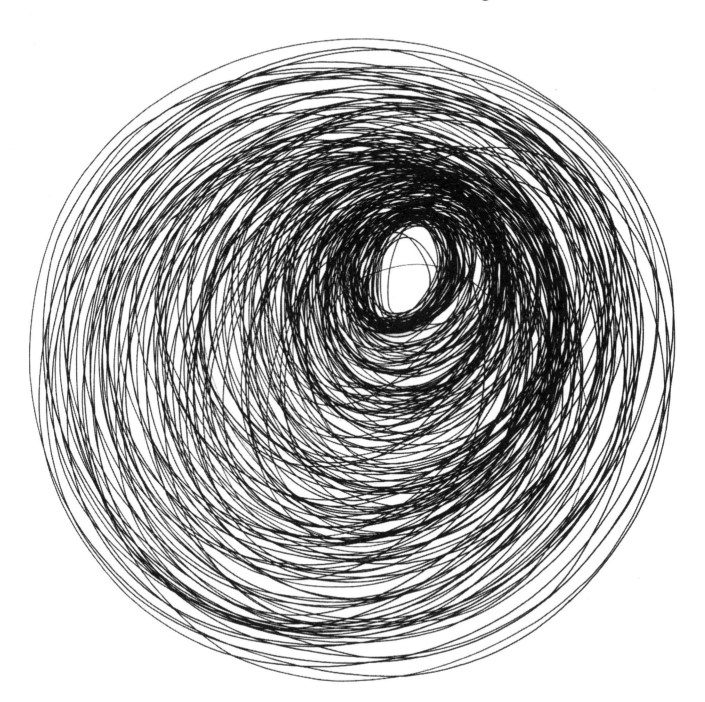

Usually scribbles are abstract.

Sometimes your scribble can become something.

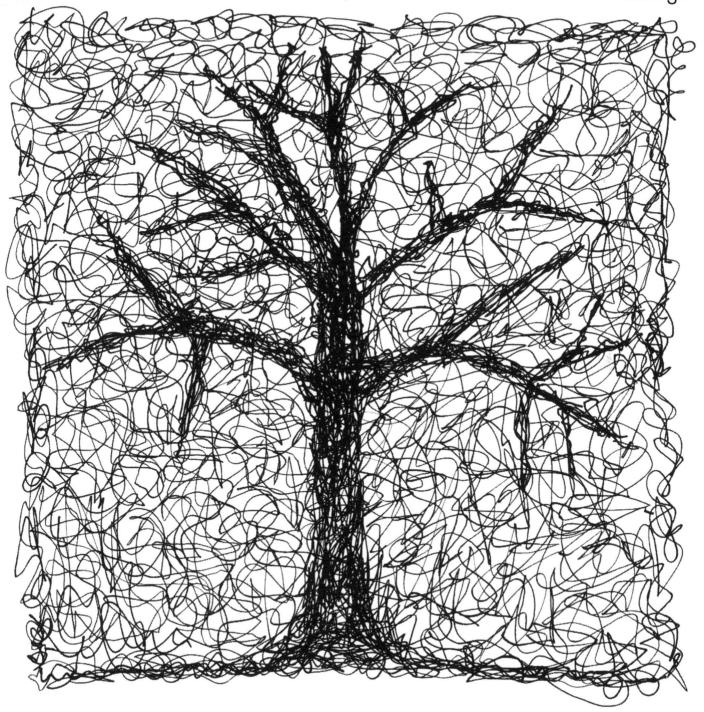

Sometimes you can find things hidden in your scribble.
Go ahead—look for images!

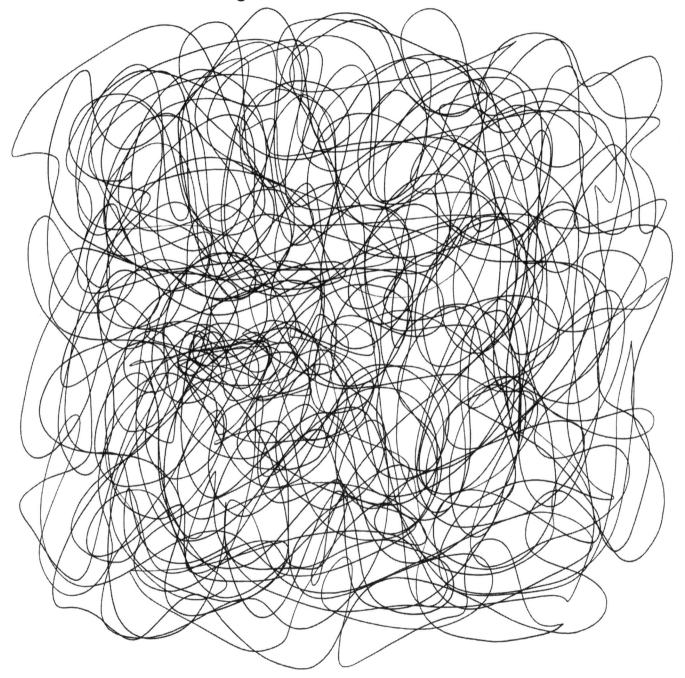

Sometimes your scribble turns into a drawing.

Your scribble is always unique.

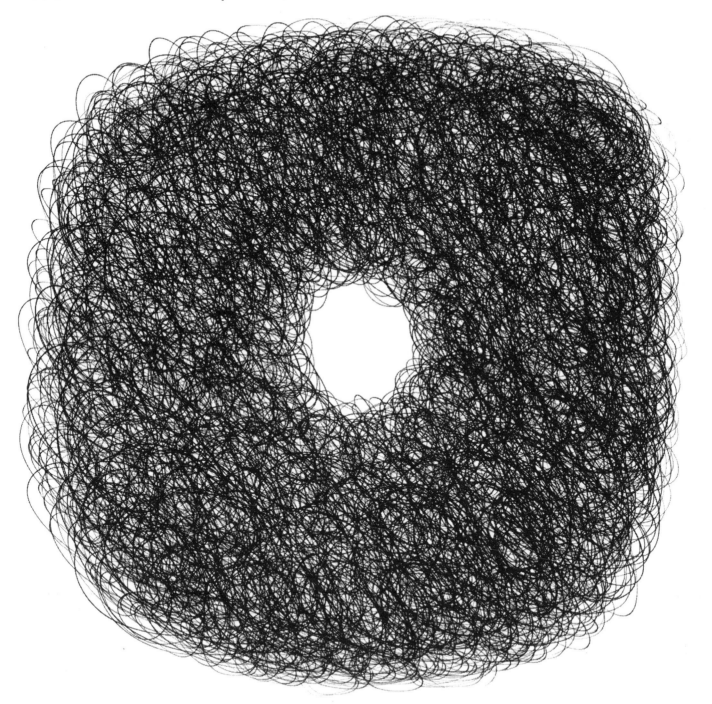

There are no two scribbles alike.

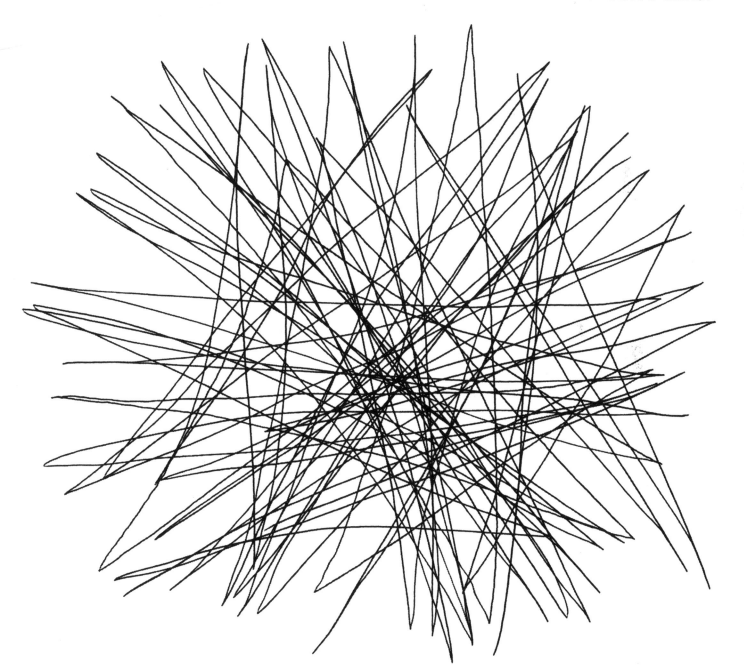

You really don't have to learn how to scribble—everyone knows how.

You might need to learn to LET GO when you scribble.
(We are not used to being given the permission to JUST scribble!)

A scribble can be like a friend.

Ready whenever you need
to pour your emotions onto a waiting page.

Or when you need some play time.

Or when you don't know what to doodle or draw.

How long do you scribble?
Scribble until you feel like you have gotten that scribble out.

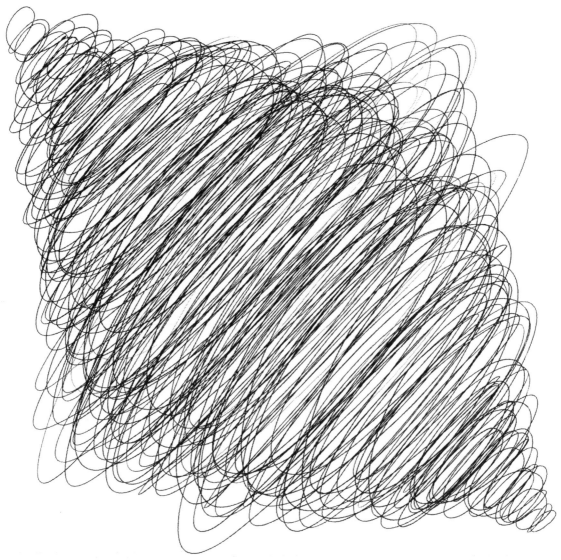

Your hand and your arm might get tired because scribbling can use
muscles you didn't know you had.
(You can tell your friends you are working out!)

Sometimes your scribble can go on all day.

Scribble in the morning
when you first get up to
shake the monkey mind.

Scribble during or after
an upsetting phone call.

Scribble before
you go to bed
to let go of any worries
or frustrations.
(It could help you
sleep better!)

Scribble when you are sick or feeling blue.

Maybe you can't get out of bed, but you can scribble.

Scribble when you are unsure of what to do next in life.

Or when you know what to do next, but it scares you.

You can also scribble how you WANT to feel.

If you are feeling anxious but you WANT
to feel peaceful, scribble the peaceful.

Or do them both.
First scribble your anxiety and then scribble your peace.

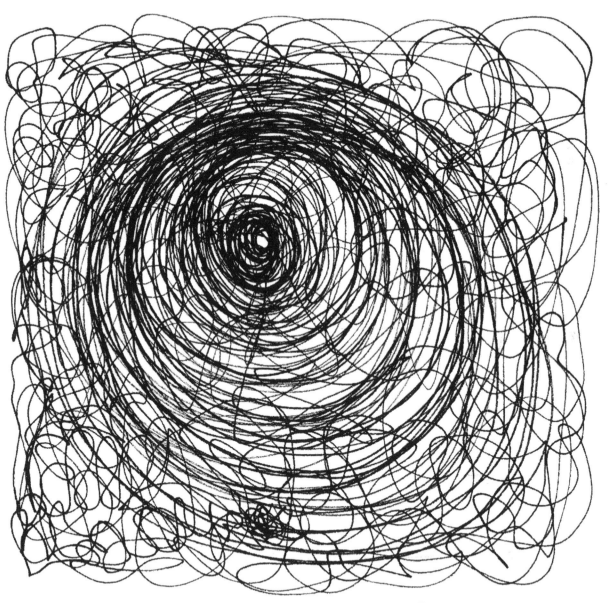

Both scribbles may want
to have a voice.

Scribble with permission NOT to think about what to scribble.

Let your scribble be
an expression.

A meditation.

A vacation from your life or thoughts.

Repetition can be enjoyable when you scribble.

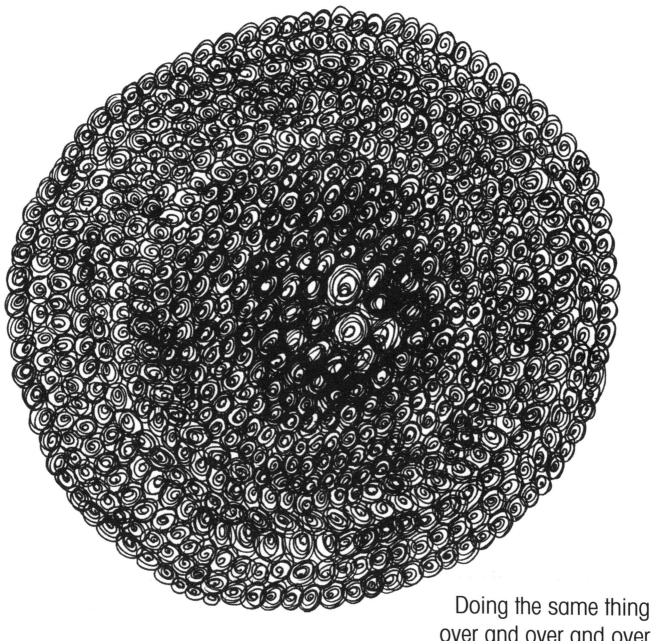

Doing the same thing
over and over and over
can be strangely comforting.

You can scribble with a ballpoint pen.
A felt tip pen.
A fancy pen.
Any pen works;
you will probably find a favorite.
Your favorite might change if you
keep scribbling.
(You can even scribble with paint or
crayons or pencil or chalk or . . .)

What do you
scribble on?

You can scribble on little paper.
Or big paper.
In a sketch book.
On cardboard.
On an envelope.
Or newspaper.
Be sure what you scribble on belongs to you!
(You can even scribble on your bills
or on the ground or in the air or . . .)

You can add words to your scribble.

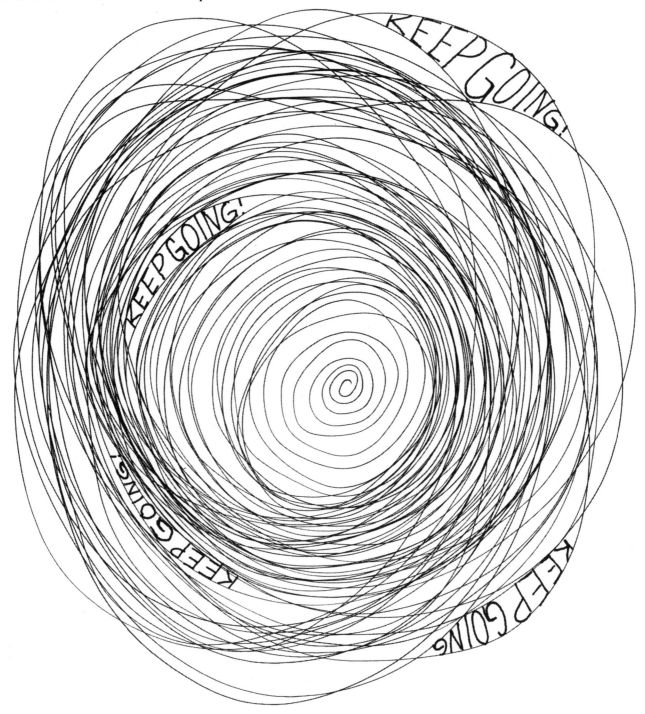

You can scribble alone or you can scribble with others.

Don't compare your scribbles,
but let other scribblers inspire you.

Sometimes your scribble can get noisy.

Sometimes your pen starts to run out of ink.

Sometimes you scribble so hard or so long it rips the paper.
(The rip WANTS to be part of your scribble.)

Don't worry about liking your scribble; remember, it is just a scribble!

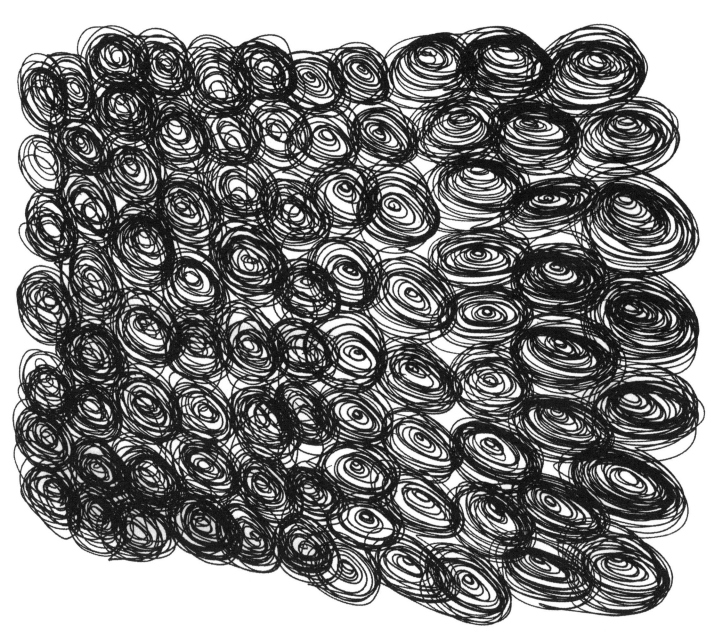

The more you scribble, the less you will care what it looks like.

If you scribble EVERY day

So reach for a pen.

And the nearest piece of paper.

Ready, set . . .

Scribble!

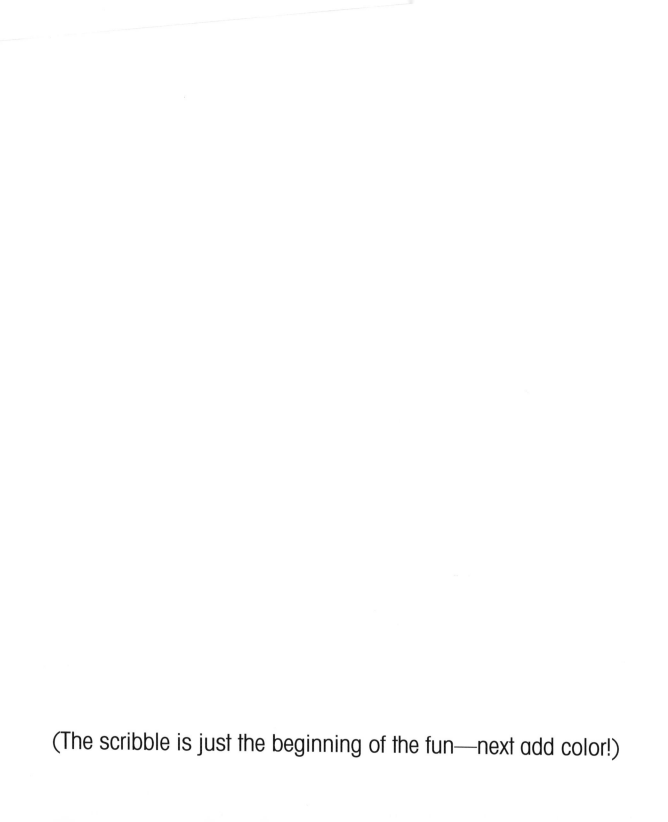

(The scribble is just the beginning of the fun—next add color!)

Do your own scribbles on these blank pages!

Do more scribbles on these blank pages—don't forget to add color!

ABOUT THE AUTHOR

Tish McAllise Sjoberg, M.A., CAGS, Expressive Arts Therapist and scribble artist, has believed since a young child that everyone can create, not just a select few. At the age of forty-four she learned about Expressive Arts Therapy, began to find her inner artist, and since, has been offering the arts to all who want it for helping and healing. Her own path to creative confidence began by finding the simplest way to jump in and overcome her fears of the blank page. The scribble is a favorite.

Tish is available for private Expressive Arts Therapy sessions and also facilitates groups, workshops, events, and on-line classes.
For more information go to
TheScribbleBook.com
and ArtHelpsArtHeals.com

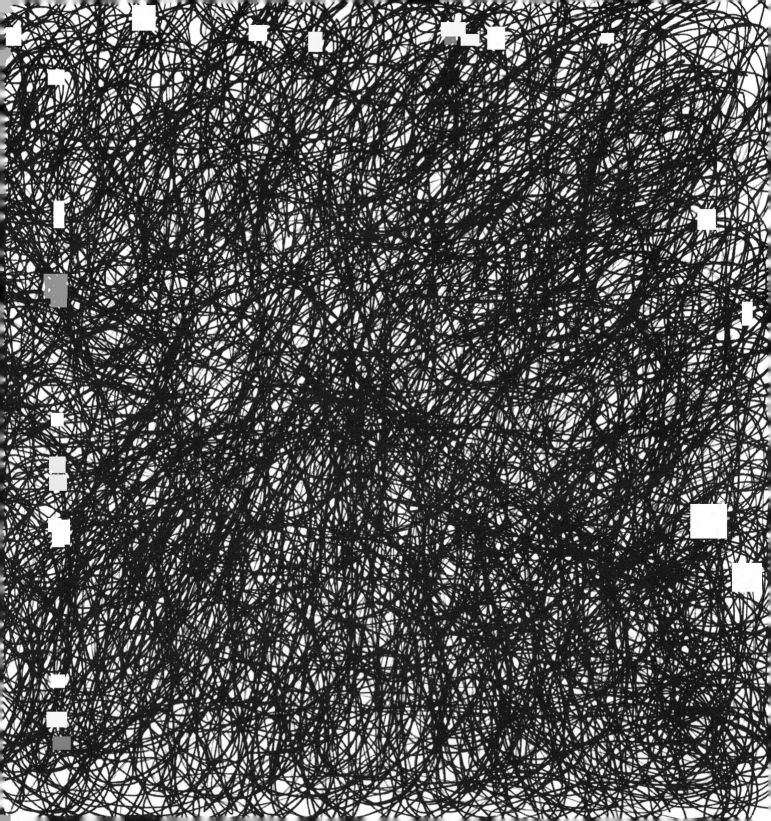

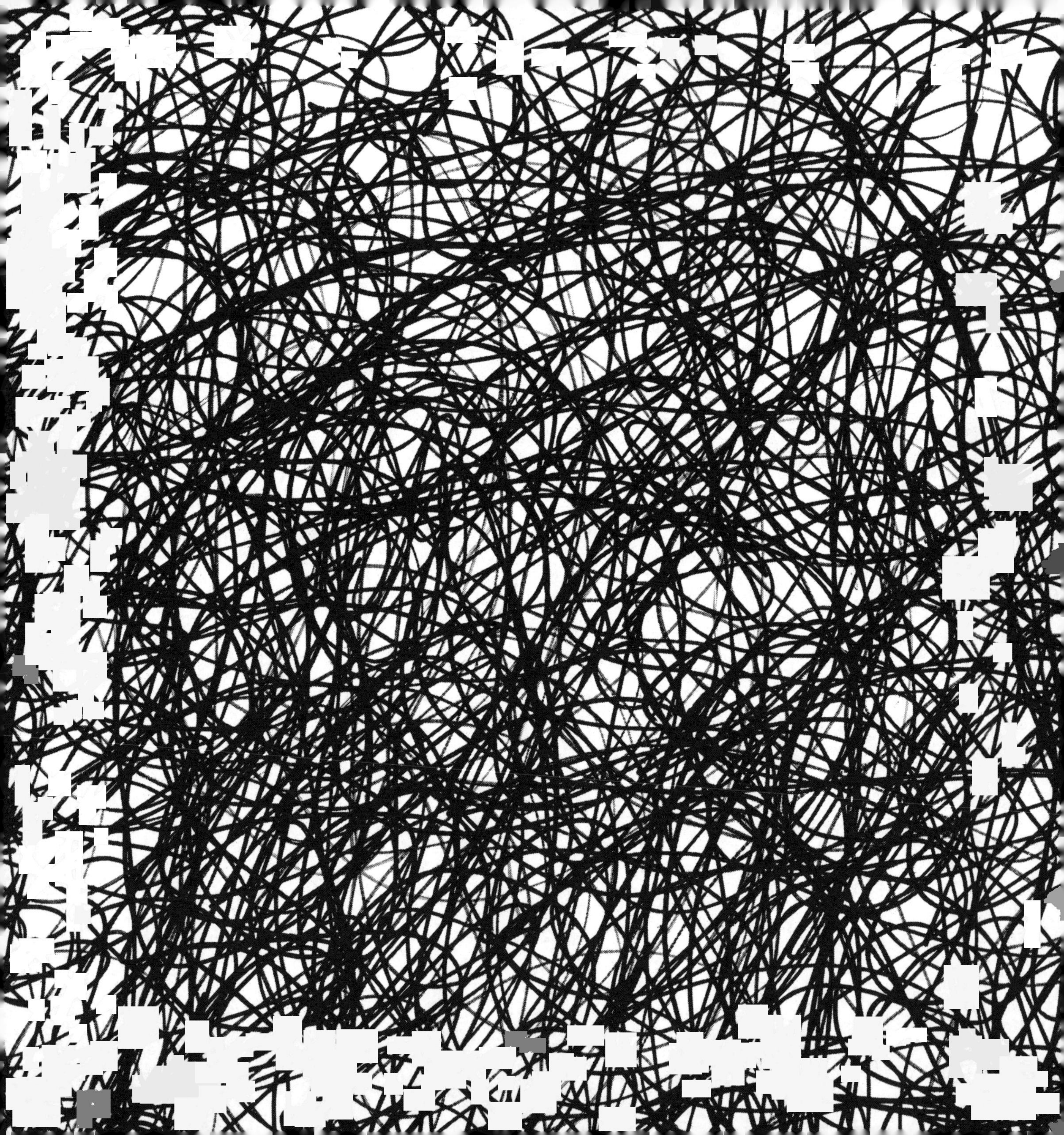

Made in the USA
Lexington, KY
28 November 2019